D0605320

I would have bought you a cat, but . . .

Other Books by Darby Conley

The Dog Is Not a Toy (House Rule #4)

Fuzzy Logic

Groovitude

The Get Fuzzy Experience

I would have bought you a cat, but . . .

A GET FUZZY *Gift Book*

Darby Conley

**Andrews McMeel
Publishing**

Kansas City

I Would Have Bought You a Cat, But . . .

03 04 05 06 07 WKT 10 9 8 7 6 5 4 3

ISBN: 0-7407-3495-4

Library of Congress Control Number: 2002116958

Attention: Schools and Businesses

Andrews McMeel books are available at quantity discounts with bulk
purchase for educational, business, or sales promotional use.
For information, please write to: Special Sales Department,
Andrews McMeel Publishing, 4520 Main Street, Kansas City, Missouri 64111.

For: Rebecca

From: Your Loverboy

Cats break things.

Cats are paranoid.

Cats are strange to outsiders.

WELL, LENNY-FROM-MEGAWORM-TELECOMMIE, YOUR LONG-DISTANCE OFFER SOUNDS FINE, BUT WHAT I'M REALLY IN THE MOOD FOR RIGHT NOW IS A BIG BOWL OF WARM FISH INTESTINES. SEE, THE GUY WHO GETS THE FOOD IN THIS HOUSE –
darb

Cats don't like dogs.

Cats have a love/hate relationship
with plants.

Cats think they run the place.

Cats are very messy.

Cats are vain.

Cats can't cook.

The object of a cat's affection
is never you.

Cats always put their needs first.

Cats don't have a sense of humor.

The only thing that matters to cats is *their* dinner.

Cats are too curious
for their own good.

Cats have over-inflated egos.

HA! YA! FA-TANG! FA-TANG! OLÉ! THIS MOVIE **ROCKS**! I WOULD BE SUCH AN AWESOME GLADIATOR! ALL I NEED IS A GOOD GLADIATOR NAME!
SWISH!

Cats have strange ways
of marking their territory.

Cats think they're smarter
than they really are.

Cats are sneaky.

You can't turn your back on a cat.

Cats are delusional.

Cats have bad breath.

Cats aren't too smart.

Cats are tactless.

Cats like to pick fights.

Cats think hugs are
personal attacks.

You can't play fetch with a cat.

Cats are finicky.

Cats have greasy paws,
but sharp claws.

Cats are always getting into things.

Cats do their own home decorating.

Cats are weird.

Cats are self-centered.

Cats have Napoleon complexes.

Cats have unrealistic expectations.

Cats are always hungry.

Cats get the midnight crazies.

And, since I really do like you,
I decided to spare you the grief.
Have a purrfect day!